Voting

Alan Trussell-Cullen

Rigby
www.Rigby.com
1-800-531-5015

Rigby Focus Forward

This Edition © 2009 Rigby, a Harcourt Education Imprint

Text © 2007 Alan Trussell-Cullen
Published in 2007 by Nelson Australia Pty Ltd ACN: 058 280 149
A Cengage Learning company

All rights reserved. No part of the material protected by this copyright may be reproduced or utilized in any form or by any means, in whole or in part, without permission in writing from the copyright owner. Requests for permission should be mailed to: Paralegal Department, 6277 Sea Harbor Drive, Orlando, FL 32887.

Rigby is a trademark of Harcourt, registered in the United States of America and/or other jurisdictions.

1 2 3 4 5 6 7 8 374 14 13 12 11 10 09 08 07
Printed and bound in China

Voting
ISBN-13   978-1-4190-3711-5
ISBN-10   1-4190-3711-0

If you have received these materials as examination copies free of charge, Rigby retains title to the materials and they may not be resold. Resale of examination copies is strictly prohibited and is illegal.

Possession of this publication in print format does not entitle users to convert this publication, or any portion of it, into electronic format.

Acknowledgments
Illustrations by Boris Silvestri
The author and publisher would like to acknowledge permission to reproduce material from the following sources:
Photographs by AAP Image/Ben Curtis, p. 15/ Alan Porritt, p. 12 bottom; Getty Images/ AFP/ Nicholas Roberts, p. 8 bottom right/ Alex Wong, p. 8 bottom left/ Photodisc Red/ Joseph Sohm-Visions of America, p. 4/ Photodisc Red/ Tom Merton, pp. 3, 10/ Reportage/ Win McNamee, p. 5; Newsphotos.com, cover, pp. 1, 9/ Andrew Brownbill, p. 10 bottom left/ Peter Kelly, p. 11, Photo Edit/ Spencer Grant, back cover; Photolibrary.com/ Photo Researchers, Inc, p. 13/ Photolibrary.com/ SuperStock, Inc/ SuperStock, p. 12 top.

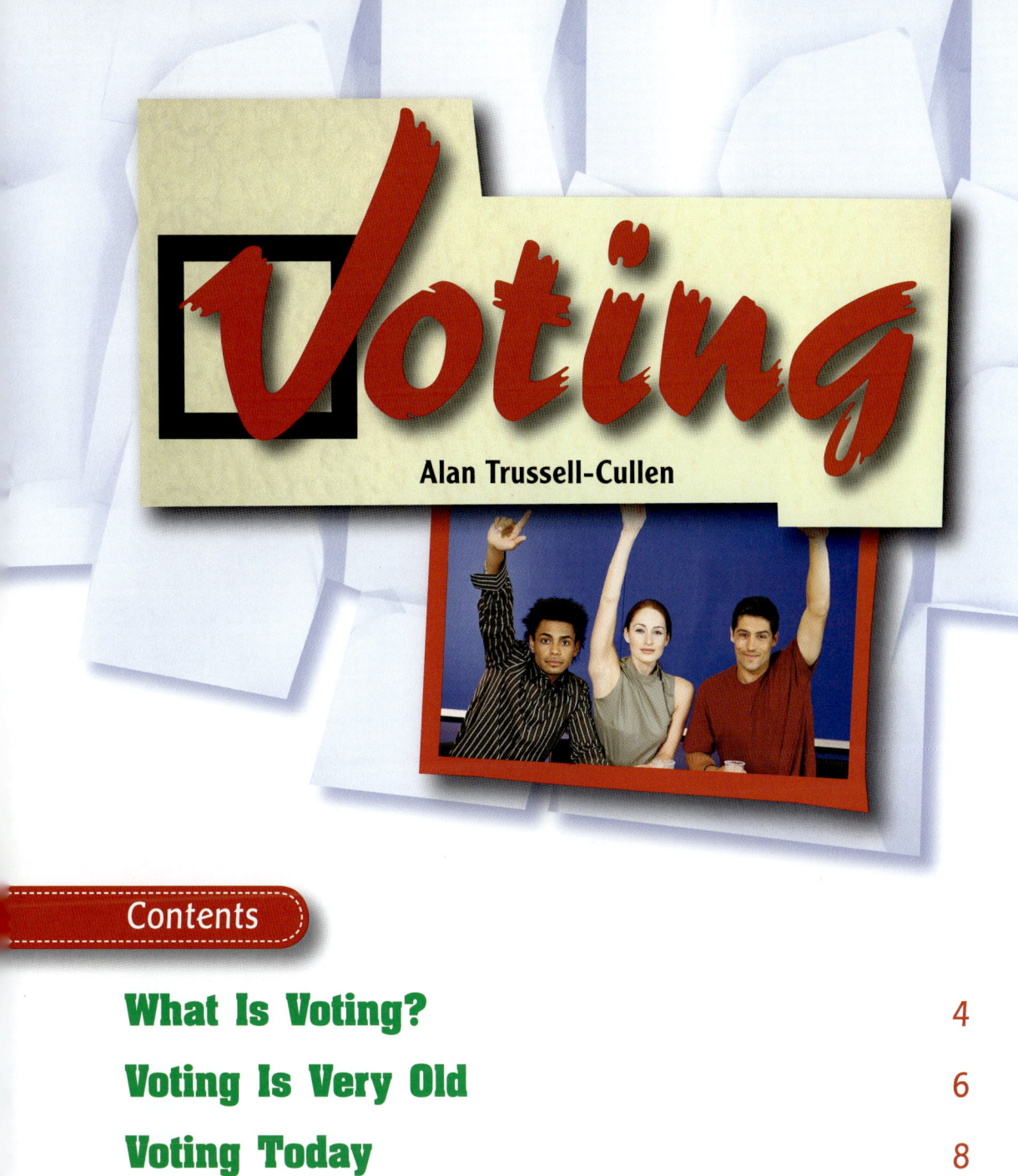

Voting

Alan Trussell-Cullen

Contents

What Is Voting? — 4

Voting Is Very Old — 6

Voting Today — 8

How Do People Vote? — 10

Who Votes? — 13

Glossary and Index — 16

WHAT IS VOTING?

Voting is when people choose something or someone they like.

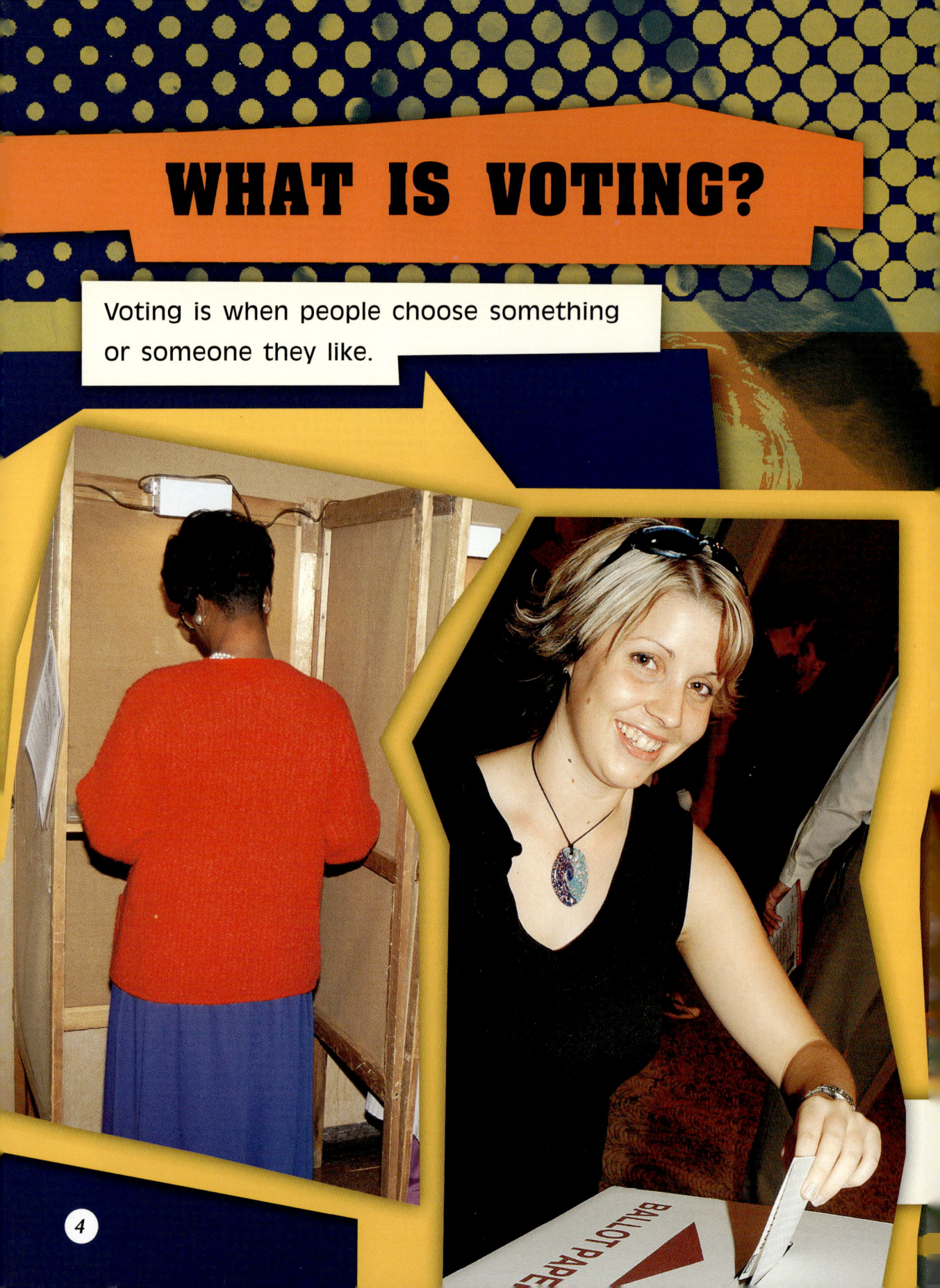

Voting gives people the right to have their say.

VOTING IS VERY OLD

People have been voting for a very long time. More than 2,000 years ago, the Greeks voted for the people they wanted to run their city.

They didn't always vote for the people they trusted. Sometimes the group had to vote for people they *didn't* want to run their city! The person who got the most votes had to leave the city!

VOTING TODAY

Today people vote for many different things. People vote to choose someone as a leader. They vote for someone to do an important job.

Nelson Mandela

George W. Bush

Hillary Clinton

They vote for what they want people to do or how they want people to do it.

They even vote for their favorite singer to win a TV competition!

HOW DO PEOPLE VOTE?

There are many ways to vote. People vote by putting up their hands.

Sometimes people don't want to tell other people who or what they voted for. It's called a **secret ballot** when people keep their vote a secret.

Paper Votes

Sometimes people write their vote on paper. Sometimes they choose from a list on paper.

WHAT DO YOU THINK IS BEST FOR THE CITY?

More buses? ☐
More cars? ☐

Please mark your choice with an "x."

Machine Votes

Sometimes people use machines to help them vote. Machines can count the votes faster than people.

Today people in some countries vote with computers.

WHO VOTES?

In some countries, leaders don't always want people to vote. These leaders don't like people telling them what to do.

Some people have had to fight for the right to vote.

Women had to fight for the right to vote.

A country where people get to choose their leader is called a **democracy**.
In a democracy, all adults have the right to vote.

Here are some countries that have a democracy.

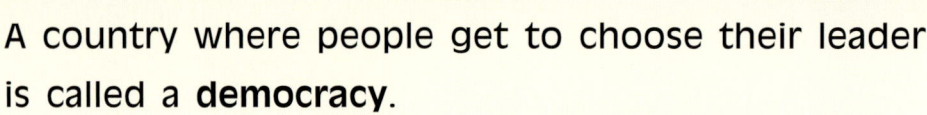

Many people think that voting is the most important right people have.

Glossary

democracy   a country where people get to vote for the leaders they want

secret ballot   when people can vote without others knowing who or what they voted for

Index

computer votes 12

Greeks 6–7

machine votes 12

secret ballot 10

women 13